WITH THESE HANDS

POETRY BY
Donna Katzin

FOREWORD BY
Archbishop Emeritus Desmond Tutu

INTRODUCTION BY
Danny Glover

MIGNON COMMUNICATIONS, LLC | NEW YORK

DEDICATION

To the children of Soweto,

and the children of tomorrow,

who give us hope and remind us

of our responsibility to pass the struggle

for a more just world from hand to hand,

from generation to generation.

Produced by Mignon Communications, LLC
www.mignoncommunications.com

Gladys Rosa-Mendoza, designer

First Edition. Published by
Mignon Communications, LLC | New York, NY 10022 | U.S.A.

Printed in China

ISBN 978-0-615-46475-6

CONTENTS

FOREWORD

Shortly after Nelson Mandela's election as South Africa's first truly democratically elected president, I commented, "The end of apartheid was Part One of the struggle. Part Two is the more difficult: To make the miracle endure." I called on friends across the globe, saying, "We asked you to disinvest. Now we say to you, invest. Make South Africa succeed. For the sake of the world."

Some took us at our word. Anti-apartheid campaigner Donna Katzin was one of them. In 1995 I remarked, "Well, Donna, I guess we've worked you out of a job!" I soon learned that Shared Interest was accompanying our people on the long path ahead to overcome generations of powerlessness and poverty, and to root the new South Africa in the soil of economic justice.

In South Africa, we have learned that the messy work of reconciliation and transformation requires accepting responsibility and seeking forgiveness for the wrongs of the past. It also requires changing them. This book, and Shared Interest's work, bear witness to that daunting task—for our people's hard labor to come to terms with our history, reimagine ourselves, and recreate our nation.

Katzin's work and Magubane's images, as well as other compelling photography, provide a window into South Africa's painful, exhilarating, and ongoing process of transformation. Ultimately they capture the power of the human spirit—the poetry of what is possible.

Archbishop Emeritus Desmond Tutu

PREFACE

After years of organizing protests and vigils, dialogues and boycotts, divestment and sanctions campaigns to press for a peaceful end to apartheid, some of us have been privileged to participate in what Archbishop Tutu calls "phase two" of the struggle—to establish South Africa's hard-won political democracy on a sustainable platform of economic justice.

Through my work at Shared Interest since 1994, the year South Africans, voting democratically for the first time, elected Nelson Mandela president, I have had the opportunity to meet and work with very remarkable "everyday" people who are on the front lines of building a new South Africa—with their own hands.

Shared Interest's partners, friends, and colleagues generously entrusted their tragedies and aspirations, challenges and dreams, in pursuing the Herculean day-to-day work of reconstructing their lives, communities, and nation.

These poems and photographs honor the mothers and fathers who have brought South Africa this far. With humility and deep appreciation, they attempt to give voice to the vision, courage, spirit of *ubuntu*, and enduring passion for justice that have so much to teach us and our world.

Donna Katzin

INTRODUCTION

"A struggle with no documentation is no struggle."

South Africa's iconic photographer Peter Magubane uttered these words in 1976 to the children of Soweto, before they trusted him with their story—and he told it, in incendiary images, to the world. The statement is no less true today than it was then. Apartheid is over. Its legacy is not. Today the inequities embedded in South Africa's economic and social fabric have fueled ongoing campaigns—still invisible to much of the world—to build a just new nation.

Our society is fast forgetting the movement that brought institutionalized racial oppression to its knees in South Africa. We know even less about the unsung communities and heroes behind today's headlines—Shared Interest's partners in South Africa since 1994—who are rebuilding their lives and their nation seed by seed, brick by brick, business by business, from the ground up.

Donna Katzin's commitment, compassion, and critical eye have characterized her work in the movement to end apartheid and then to replace it with a more equitable South Africa. As a participant and writer, she opens a powerful portal for us with her conversation in poetry and photography. This work reflects South Africa's own inexhaustible capacity to imagine and give birth to itself.

As the next leg of South Africa's journey unfolds, this conversation welcomes all participants—struggle pioneers and new partners, those who are leading and learning the way, and those who will come after.

Danny Glover

The old fort stands,

a cathedral on the heights

where Braamfontein meets Hillbrow and Houghton,

a reverent marker on the journey

from terror to transformation.

In the African night

silver moons shine

like the scales of justice.

FROM THESE SEEDS

Robben Island

A rough outcropping gleams
   on blue sea skin—
a necklace or a knife.
Gone are storms
that once shook the island.
Beneath the surface,
green veins of kelp float
   from the mainland
like memory.

The prison built by captives
from its own grey granite
for lepers and inmates
calls to be remembered
   in seagulls' sobs
and whispers.

Just past dawn,
waves still wash the beaches clean
of blood and longing,
leaving fragments of shell and
   bone
stripped bare like castigated
   prisoners
in the carnivorous wind.

A colony of penguins
black and white
flap flightless wings
before slipping into surf
like shooting stars
in liquid sky.

At the limestone pit, a pile of rocks
abrasive, smooth, imposing, shy,
the hues of earth, night
   and endless days,
recalls insistent picks
   and patient hands
that quarried building blocks
of the new nation.

A grey moth flutters between
   the bars
like a spent spirit
seeking light
in empty cells.

An iron key struggles to release
    the lock
that grits its teeth,
opening a sacred space
barely big enough for a man,
his cup, plate,
bucket and blanket
on the unforgiving floor.

Ahmed's bench still leans
against the wall
where he stood
and stared beyond slim slits
to get a glimpse of gulls
and children.

Mbeki
Mhlaba
Mlangeni
Motsoaledi,
Kathrada,
Sisulu,
Mandela...
Morning's roll call hangs in the air
like an unrequited noose.

Even now,
fluorescent eyes that never close
invade the cells
looking for the ghosts
of greatness.

These years later
echoing back across the sea
the gift of song.

17

To Robben Island's Children

In darkness
you wake and liberate
your captive toes, like doves,
into the frozen morning.

Every day you squint
across cruel waves
at the city winking at you
like a forbidden jewel.

When no one is looking,
you scribe your name on stones
in a cold chronicle
of your own blood.

Beneath the bare bulb
you study the language of the jailor,
dreaming one day
it will set you free.

You write letters that may not pass the censors
twice a year, as authorized,
to sons and daughters
who may not answer.

Joyfully you welcome prisoners
to the island
as if it were a family
or a ferry to freedom.

Gathering each human strand,
you knit nets stronger
than the chains
and prison walls.

You break limestone
with dull hammers
and blistered hands,
forging tools to govern.

Then, heart thundering,
decades later, you step steady, stride out
into a land that has changed,
but not enough.

With dimming eyes, you strain
to craft a constitution
for generations you will not know,
enshrining rights you have only imagined.

Remember with shame the many thousands of people who lived for generations in District 6 and other parts of the city, and were forced by law to leave their homes because of the colour of their skins. FATHER, FORGIVE US.
—Plaque of Shame
(outside the District 6 Museum)

District 6

In the shadow of Table Mountain,
between fragmented stones and broken glass,
the feinbos pushes up its heads,
erupts in feathers of dusk and dawn,
sprinkles seeds
when no one is looking.

In an unassuming corner of the site,
Kalam Construction squeezes concrete
from steel tubes into rectangular foundations
for new families,
and a few removed to Nyanga, Manenberg
    and Mitchell's Plain
who remember the bulldozers that leveled
    District 6,
renamed it Zonnebloem.

Noor invites the guests to his safe haven
for rollers, razors, bottle caps,
pieces of a jigsaw puzzle entitled "Cottages,"
between a flower and candle,
a drawing from Nomvuyo's long-demolished
    room—
"God Bless our Home."

From the walls, the Paramount Dance Band
and Willie's Starlite Orchestra play on—
drums, saxophones, accordions
silenced in their prime, along with
church bells,
Kol Nidre,
the call to prayer.

On the floor map
former residents reinsert their names
into the alleys, avenues taken from them:
Aspeling
Barrack
Constitution
Darling
Frere
Stuckeris
Tennant
Upper Ashley

Street signs rescued by a demolition worker
on the trellis of remembrance.

Noor closes his eyes,
revisits the plot on Caledon Street
where his house once stood,
finds the fifty pigeons he tried to retrain
to return to Athlone.
They stare at him but do not move.
To them this is home.

Requiem

The hard-packed land

holds a man too big

to be confined to a cell

or the back of a truck,

too alive to lie beneath the earth—

a man who folded his people

in a resplendent blanket of blackness

stitched with shivering stars.

A great stone stretches out,

surrounded by oceans of pebbles

in dry ground.

Soft shells curl around the dawn

like flowers of the sea

on the grave of Stephen Biko.

Soweto

Forty, or perhaps a hundred years ago today
                  at Morris Isaacson
       we jostle joyous
              unruly   angry
waving signs refusing
     instruction in the language
            of the oppressor.

     We hold hands, little ones close,
march and toyi-toyi
     writing our demands on dusty paths
          with our feet
then with our blood.

          Hot metal shatters morning.
Our mothers sing "Senzeni na?"
           "Senzeni na."

     In the garden
     of the Hector Petersen Museum
stones scattered by the hundreds
  bear our names

       Anonymous
            Anonymous
  Anonymous

The Price
of Freedom
for Ashley Kriel

Where would you be today
if they had not hammered your young wings?

Your flat belly stuffed with dreams,
would it be extra baggage now?
Would your tiny house in Bonteheuvel,
whose beds could barely breathe between the
    walls,
be the dim memory of a mansion
in Houghton?

Would the comets in your eyes
cloud behind wire frames?
Would you be baptizing your son?
Running a ministry?
Would your mother have worn a bright shawl
to your swearing-in, instead of sewing
your shroud?

for Ivy Kriel

You had not seen it coming—
the slow cyclone that ripped through
   Bonteuheuvel
lashing its long tail in pain
behind the casket
of your son.

You had not seen it coming on the job
serving tea to corporates
dabbing their white lips
with serviettes,
asking you please
for a bit more milk.

You never saw a scrap
of black and green and gold
as you stitched quilts
from daughters' outgrown dresses
and your spent skirts,
two decades old,
that had given up on their own.

You had not seen it all those nights
when quiet Ashley did not make it home,
stayed with friends in the township,
came for a change of clothes
in the morning.
That's the way things were
in those days.

Even when they told you,
"student leader," "freedom fighter"
sounded foreign—
could not apply to your good boy
who helped you with the chores,
protected you with gentle manners
and his silence.

What could you have done
when policemen came in uniform,
threw his slender shirted body
   to the floor,
put a gun to his head,
took the boy that you loved most,
for whom you labored all your life,
without even asking?

The question never left you.
It clattered in the teacups,
chanted with the comrades,
toyi-toyied at all hours
in the dusty streets of the township
to the last beat of your tired heart
the night it broke.

Imbokodo

Fifty years later
she begins again.
She has marched
    these streets before.
She has never set foot on them.
Bent with years of service, silence
    and resistance
she toyi-toyis like a young girl,
her thin dress dancing
    in the winter wind.

She joins rivers of her sisters—
sinuous streams of bright beads,
    braids,
currents of green, gold and black,
willed by banner sails
scribed with prophecy
half a century old:
*Now that you have touched
    the women,*
you have struck a rock.

On resonant stone
her feet drum praise songs
to the women of the townships,
    fields,
shacks, the madam's house,

drum to unions, Women's League,
churches, stokvels,
drum to the prisons
drum now the corridors of
    parliament.

She has stitched together
    too many mornings
waiting for news
that does not come,
washed too many bodies
wasted by apartheid and AIDS,
gathered flowers
    for too many funerals,
tucked too many futures
    of the nation
into pine boxes.

Her voice soars once again
in sunrise cadences
of "Senzeni na,"
beyond the shadow-mouthed
    monsters
who invade her nights,
leaving bruises on her back
and deep blue valleys beneath
    the eyes
where stars once shone.

In her mind
she draws water
from the deep taciturn well
that turns in on itself
in the dry season,
and capricious communal tap
that speaks in fits and starts,
stuttering life into plastic bottles.

She draws strength
from mothers who led the way,
bundles on their backs
and in their arms,
with no shoes,
no bus fare, no map,
only petitions and prayers,
tornadoes in their hearts.

She is Lillian,
Rahima, Helen and Sophie,
Victoria, Albertina and Phumzile,
measuring history with small steps
on impervious paths and pavement
to take their place
in their people's march to freedom.
They are still marching.

On August 9, 2006, South Africa's women reenacted the march to Pretoria's Union Buildings that more than 20,000 staged 50 years earlier to protest the application of the hated apartheid pass laws to women. The march theme, which has survived, is *"Watint' abafazi, wathint' imbokodo"*—"Now that you have touched the women, you have struck a rock."

WITH THESE HANDS

Crossroads

Wind pries cold claws

through matchbox cracks

between boards and tin,

pushes aside bits of newspaper and plastic
stuffed against the night,

sucks up breaths

that hang heavy in the air

like the angel of death.

The paraffin is spent.

Blankets fall away like wasted skin.

Thabi stands guard
over her children,

listening for the neighbors shouting *fire*,

waiting for dawn.

Madolo flies
on hammer hooves of driven wind,
shirt rippling like a freedom flag,
his face the color of the open turf.

Across the road
dust settles in Marconi Beam,
where Mrs. Madolo towers
like Table Mountain,
pick ax in hand.
It rises, falls,
rises, falls,
separates sod,

reclaims foundations.
She is digging
for her family's brick house
that will withstand the Cape gales
before winter hardens the ground
and rains insinuate themselves
between the boards and plastic
she has put between her family
and the storms.

In her whirlwind memory
police are tearing down her shack,
issuing cold edicts in Afrikaans.
"Kaffirs" cannot live here.
She is the wrong color.
She cannot stay
   with her jockey-love
who is riding, riding

Eyes ahead, Madolo flies.
He will have his house.
Tomorrow he will own
   the horse
and the land...

Milnerton Turf Club,
1996

Khayelitsha

She stands beside her pile
     of bricks,

    a sixty-rand cement bag in her hand,

        strokes smooth concrete
that will unite these blocks

    into warm walls closing out the winds.

    Here her children will dry their feet in winter,

       do their sums to bulbs,

  not paraffin.

She will sleep deeply

  and dream of planting

    her garden.

Ma May

In her hands
bottles come alive.
Around the plastic torsos
swelling bosoms and bums
take shape beneath cloth
conjured by Nomalizo.
She hums and wraps
the shy brides
in rainbow skirts
stitched by Nosimpiwe
and beaded blankets
that hold them close in
the Khayelitsha winds.
She and Rose Siyanga
crown stocking faces
with bright scarves,
smooth their midnight hair
and spangle them with galaxies
of jubilant earrings and necklaces
until they are ready.

For a moment
she caresses them
like daughters
lost to AIDS,
and granddaughters
who must stand strong
in new homes and take
their rightful place
in this land.

Annunciation

In the rolling valley of the Fish River

bright aloes flame

from green brush,

igniting hopes of scattered shacks

with burning bush tongues

and the sweetness of healing.

Franschhoek

At dawn
on a white-owned farm,
Andreis starts the sprinklers,
showers thirsting tendrils
with shimmering sheets
of new life.

Pulsing in the reservoir below,
his own quivering fingerlings
feed on his formula.

His face shines like a dark moon.
Its craggy craters ripple out
across the landscape
of white men's vines
and black men's dreams.

He waves away the circling cormorants
eyeing breakfast
just below the surface
and hovering
like apartheid ghosts
waiting for a tear in the nets.

From a tin bucket
he nourishes his trout
with fistfuls of feed
that hang in the Cape mist
like manna from heaven.

Umtata

Bricks and boards
cling to each other
in the twisted twilight
between disrepair
and despair
reclaiming the right
to hold back winds
until morning.

She coughs blood, but will not take
   her AZT today.
Only the sickest get grants,
as school fees come knocking
at the door,
and the mealie meal
has run out.

She hurries her smallest one to class.
His feet drum urgent rhythms
on dirt paths,
as wind wings through his primer
unfurls the flags of his uniform
and whispers sentences and sums—
the dust in its mouth
echoing his name.

Far away a father
scratches at the scabby skin of the city
for a job
a bowl of pap
a bottle of beer
a pair of shoes
a dream to dream
and a ticket home.

Ostriches

It is spring in Pikoli of the old Ciskei.
New farmers struggle
to lift the curse of "Bantustan"
from the place where their families were
   discarded,
scraped from the soil
of their birth.

With no children, young Melumzi
and his mother, Nelindile,
open arms to embrace new chicks
and place them,
kahle kahle,
in the small house of clay
that will be their home.

The two kneel
and click insistent fingers
on feed trays
until the young chicks copy
with tiny beaks
and peck their first grains.

Cold, a stealthy predator,
creeps into the pen.
Nelindile gathers up newborns
in the arms of wooden rings,
and covers them with blankets
from her own bed.

The two stay with the little ones,
holding and singing to them softly
until night has settled in
and they are no longer afraid.

XDR-TB
After the Jose Pearson Hospital

In Port Elizabeth
dawn steals through
   the barbed fence
past the guard
still dozing.

A jailor in white makes rounds
clinking keys and pills
to banish the invisible beast
that prowls the corridors
and preys on patients
as they sleep.

Recurring nightmares shake Ntsiki
with shouts and crowbar hands
that pry her from her shack
in the middle of the night.

She is awakened by the cough
that draws blood from her chest.
It holds her close
and will not let go.

Today her children come.
Themba, taller now,
incarcerates his own secrets
in the prison of his heart.
Naledi pretends himself a garden
of sweet mangos and cool shade,
and will not meet her hungry eyes.
Small Lerato, taken at birth,
does not even remember
her name.

Through windows in the razor wire,
her butterfly lungs
wing their way
to freedom.

Orchard

With gnarled fingers
Agnes twists the firm red flesh,
its tight skin mirroring ardor
that birthed her children
and her dreams.

She coaxes branches
calling forth their offspring—
Pink Lady, Royal Gala, Granny Smith, Sundowner—
to take their places at the courts of Europe
and tables of the nation.

Her trunk thick with years
has withstood storms
of hail, men
and a country that saw her
only as a shadow.

Rooted in deep soil,
veiled in mist—
one great tree
among the seedlings.

Oukasie

Mist hangs over frozen fields

heavy with spirits.

Themba's dark wood voice draws power

from a deep drum,

calls seedlings to stand straight,

bear blossoms.

They sip dew

and spill perfume

across the waking land.

Mushrooms

In darkness and dampness,
day after day,
Neo tends the silent spores
meditating in compost pews
beneath the peat.

She and her sisters
guide trays from room
to room,
watch
wait
wonder.

As dawn cracks
the sixteenth day,
she dons white robes,
quiets her heart
and measures her steps
to the final chamber .

There
multitudes
a million strong
raise shiny white capped heads
in a chorus of bright
hosanahs.

Bless

His hand hangs

across his mother's neck.

He clings to her

stretched across her back

in earth-tone shroud

a bundle of bones.

The lost stars of his eyes cry out

dry wells

pleading for rain.

Egoli

In the pale haze of the City of Gold,

        mountains of dust glow—

monuments to overseers

        and armies of black workers forced to dig mines

        and their own graves.

Legacy:

        mounds of mineral detritus

        widows

        a trace of arsenic in the air.

Lerato's Lullaby

Her sister sleeps, but she must not.
Between the bolted boards, she listens for
the hiss of the Jukskei,
restless serpent of Alexandra.

Between the bolted boards, she listens for
warning shouts, torches in the shadows.
The restless serpent of Alexandra
consumed five shacks only last night.

Warning shouts, torches in the shadows—
too late to save Nonhlanhla and Siphiwe,
consumed with their shacks only last night
when the moon went blind.

Too late to save Nonhlanhla and Siphiwe,
the other children watched them float away
when the moon went blind.
Mama and Tata dreamed of a house on the hill.

The other children watched them float away
beside the hungry mud and empty bottles.
Mama and Tata dreamed of a house on the hill
to the dim drumming of the rain.

Beside the hungry mud and empty bottles,
her sister sleeps but she must not
to the dim drumming of the rain,
the hiss of the Jukskei.

He Is Not Coming Home to Bulawayo

He will not kick another ball

past his barefoot brother,

call to girls who ripple by

in ribbons and beads,

haunt the market for a job,

promise his mother mealies and mangoes

from across the border.

In Alex, his shack smolders

with the heart cut out.

He lies beside it

in takkies that could not run

fast enough.

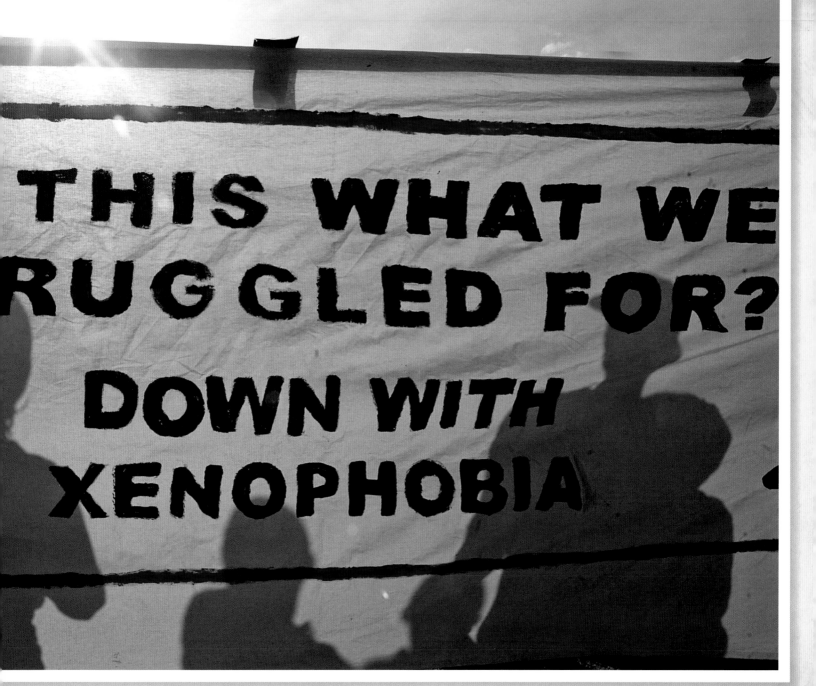

Living River

On Sunday in Thembisa,
as August's chill consumes the congregation,
Mrs. Sibiya in her cotton dress
and children in torn tee shirts shiver in the back pews.
It was warmer in Harare.

Others, in jerseys and jackets,
keep their eyes on the pastor,
but take note of new guests.
After services they flush out drawers,
salvage long-sleeve shirts and woolen wraps,
prepare parcels.

On Wednesday, as the small brick structure struggles
to support its timbers,
newcomers without papers look quickly left,
right and back again,
discern smiles, gestures—
"You can come."

First the soup—veggies with a bit of meat,
rice, brown bread, tea, scones.
Mrs. Radebe places a shawl on thin shoulders,
folds the boy into a coat only a little too large,
weaves the streams from south and north together—
one river.

Atterbury Road

Beneath her mushroom hat,

she bustles over baking concrete,

parcel in hand,

purse tight under her arm,

sways to avoid the Toyota

that beeps her out of the slipway.

From her bag,

ripe mangoes for Madam pour perfume

sweet as Zanele's and Malumi's sticky kisses before school.

She hums a hymn

smooth as blue gum honey for the tea,

waits behind the yellow line for the bus

that doesn't come.

Essie Mulapo

Across the stubble of pale veld
    the color of bush tea
        she follows her shrinking shadow
    leaving soft prints in soil
she will sculpt
    into smooth vessels.

She will ask the chief for bags of earth
    alive with ancestors who inhabit the land,
      carry it home,
        kahle kahle,
    coaxing it into pots
to feed the living.

    The ritual is as old as the winds of Mashishing.
But the strong lines she traces in the clay
    will be her own.

Rifilwe's Garden

She sags beneath the cement bag half her size—

a slim stem with too big a blossom—

picks her stony path beside the Magalies River

to the shack of her mother.

She steps across the markers planted in the ground.

Neat squares declare foundations

for the house that will learn to stand up to the battering wind

one brick at a time.

Siboshwa

Tonga, Mpumalanga.

Baby monkeys lope across the road.

A cow scratches her chin on a broken stump.

The river curls like a snake

sleeping in the fields.

Nomsa Zitha

Sbongile Mashala

Jeni Manoka

Sisi Sibiya

Lindiwe Mhlongo,

hoes in hand,

ripple through their furrows,

bringing life

to red soil.

Isaac bumps his bicycle
over sand and stones,

his hair a white wool cap
hugging an ancient mountain.

From his spare pole frame

his shirt waves

to the cool sky

watching him.

After years of mixing chemicals
in Johannesburg

he has come home

to tend the generation of new cane

that curtsies to greet him

and stretches strong sweet leaves

to the sun.

Sibongile

Beside the Komati River,
she gives thanks,
parts curtains of cane
she has planted in red soil,
nurtured to maturity with her own hands,
and steps into the furrows of their sanctuary.

Now fully grown,
slender stalks tower over her.
They see beyond the green waves
to the mill that will milk their sweetness
into white gold.

In the cool Mpumalanga morning
they whisper.
There, in the temple of her heart,
she listens to the beat of the earth,
reclaims her right to dream.

The Training

In the shadow of the great acacia,

beneath black clouds pregnant with blessings,

the women put babies to breast,

wait on woven lavender, vermillion.

Asphinah welcomes them to plant businesses,

work as fingers of one hand

with friendship of the palm,

power of the fist.

What kind of leaders will you be?

not the roaring lion who does not listen.

And the giraffe with her head in the sky?

She cannot live without the water of the ground.

A Mountain in Winter

Dora tightens her torn blanket

stuffed with duvets, bedspreads

and embroidered cotton curtains

for pensioners and teachers, steps

between dry bushes and bare rocks,

dreams herself a spaza, then a shop.

Cold lashes like razor wire. Dust snaps at her ankles,

swarms in her eyes. Sand grinds in the teeth of the wind.

Anna Mhlambi

In the dim garage

they smooth the leaves of savings books

seeded with dreams

to package diapers, sew curtains,

distribute oranges and avos,

open spazas, shelter orphans.

Edith's toddler tickles her shoulder.

Wrapped in saffron, azure, Leah calls the Creator.

Anna rises like a sun,

warms the huddled women

with a hymn.

Her smile awakens their gardens.

Ipopeng

Black women bustle with
   anticipation
infants and bundles on their backs
savings books in hand,
greet each other,
squeeze themselves
into the spare garage.
Latecomers will be fined.
They make space on spare benches,
gather expectantly.

The chairlady signals.
They becomes an instant choir
filling the space with
   rich harmonies
and rhythms of mbilas.

Heads incline. Eyes close.
The wizened woman
in grey and brown knit cap calls
Come Spirit,
bless this meeting,
give us strength to sustain
   those who depend on us,
give us courage,
give us life.
Amen.

Eyes fix forward
on the leaders at the front
who pledge to carry out
   the covenants,
share the single breath that
   nurtures all.
They introduce the visitors—
"Tobela," I say,
"Tobela," they answer.
We are ready.

Each group leader brings offerings—
worn coins, carefully folded notes
saved, borrowed, repaid.
The treasurer counts, recounts.
Every pair of eyes counts with her.
Anna Baloyi. *"Ten rand."*
Applause.
Virginia Mogale. *"Twenty-eight*
   rand."
Applause.
Mumsy Malema. *"Seventy-four*
   rand."
Applause.
Caroline Makgobathou. *"One*
   hundred thirty rand."
Applause...

Tsholo wriggles from a lap
takes his first step-steps,
grips strong, slim fingers
extended by the many mothers.

Josefina scribes the numbers
in each cardboard loan and
   savings book—
precious currency
invested in each other,
mealie meal, stock for sale,
school fees, university...

With closing prayer,
the assembly spills out
   into the dry day,
Caroline taking up her rusty
   wheelbarrow overflowing with
   maize snacks
for children after class,
Mumsy bearing bags of guava juice.

They ripple down the sandy road
in sun-soaked, earth-red,
   sea-green skirts
with a splash of laughter.

Homecoming

Lush blades ululate
      in celebration,
   welcoming their people home.

      Many suns have slid behind the hills
since pale men came with trucks and guns,
   tore families from the soil,
         and scattered them
   like seeds in the wind.

Clouds whisper blessings,
   drape soft shawls
      over earth's brown bosom.

   Striding down sleek slopes
the Makhoba come
     to reclaim their land
   and make it sing.

GLOSSARY

Albertina Sisulu – a political activist from her youth, a deeply respected leader through bitter years of repression, elected first president of the United Democratic Front in 1983, wife of renowned African National Congress leader Walter Sisulu and loved as a "Mother of the Nation"

Alex – short for Alexandra (township)—site of anti-immigrant violence, a primarily black area outside Johannesburg, immediately adjacent to one of South Africa's wealthiest suburbs, Sandton

ANC – African National Congress

Apartheid – denied "Africans" political and economic and personal rights, such as the right to own land, or to move freely from one place to another; under apartheid, areas of land to which Africans had been restricted in colonial times, known as Reserves, were reclassified as Bantustans, as part of an attempt to justify to an international audience African exclusion from full participation in all of South Africa

Ashley Kriel – an ANC youth leader in the Western Cape during the 1980s, brutally murdered by apartheid police at the age of nineteen

Bantustan – impoverished areas to which black South Africans (as Africans were classified during apartheid) were relegated by ethnicity

Bonteheuvel – a historically mixed-race township outside of Cape Town

Braamfontein – a neighborhood in Johannesburg

Bulawayo – the second largest city in Zimbabwe

Ciskei – One of the designated "Bantustans" in the Eastern Cape

District 6 – a multiracial community in the heart of Cape Town that was destroyed and its 60,000 residents removed by apartheid authorities during the 1970s; to date, most of the area remains vacant land

Egoli – Johannesburg (in Zulu: "Place of Gold")

Feinbos – the wild vegetation that thrives in parts of the Western Cape ("fine bush" in Afrikaans)

Franschhoek – a town in the heart of the winelands outside of Cape Town

Hillbrow – a high-rise, now mixed working-class neighborhood in Johannesburg

Houghton – a wealthy Johannesburg residential area

Imbokodo – "rock" in Zulu

Jukskei – the river that runs through Alexandra

Jose Pearson Hospital – a tuberculosis hospital operated by the South African government, to which patients with extremely drug resistant tuberculosis (XDR-TB) are confined, often against their will

Kahle kahle – "gently gently" in Xhosa

Kaffir – a derogatory racial slur, historically used in South Africa as "nigger" was in the United States

Khayelitsha – a township outside of Cape Town, historically designated for blacks, (means "our homes" in Xhosa)

Lillian Ngoyi, Rahima Moosa, Helen Joseph, Sophie Williams de Bruyn – the four women who presented the women's petitions at Prime Minister Strijdom's offices on August 9, 1956

Makhoba – Makhoba people were forcibly removed from their land in 1946 and only returned after a successful petition to the Land Claims Court in 1996; since then they have struggled to support their 1,400 families on the land, where they are now growing commercial grain

Manenburg – a mixed-race township outside of Cape Town

Mashishing – a town in the province of Mpumalanga

Mbilas – traditional wooden percussion instruments

Mealies – corn

Milnerton Turf Club – a racetrack on the outskirts of Cape Town; for thirty years before the end of apartheid, South African authorities applied the Group Areas Act to prohibit black families from living with their husbands and fathers who worked at the racecourse

Mitchell's Plain – a mixed race township outside of Cape Town

Mpumalanga – South Africa's eastern province that borders Swaziland and Mozambique ("land of the rising sun" in Swazi)

Nyanga – a black township outside of Cape Town

Phumzile Mlambo-Ngcuka – deputy president of South Africa from 2005 to 2008

Robben Island – the island prison where Nelson Mandela and many other black leaders and activists were imprisoned during apartheid

Senzeni Na – a song sung as the women presented their petitions to the government officials, and throughout the anti-apartheid movement; means "What have we done?"

Sibongile – a popular name, meaning "Thank you, God" in Zulu

Soweto – originally short for South West Township; on June 16, 1976, black children in Soweto were shot by apartheid police when they protested the edict that all instruction would be in Afrikaans; they gathered at Morris Isaacson High School; Hector Petersen is remembered as the first child to die in the Soweto massacre; a small museum in the township bears his name

Stephen Biko – one of South Africa's leading black consciousness movement leaders, murdered by apartheid police in 1977 at the age of thirty

Takkies – sneakers

Thembisa – a black working-class community just outside of Johannesburg

Toyi-toyi – traditional march-dance done by anti-apartheid protesters

Ubuntu – the concept that a person cannot be fully human in isolation from the humanity of others; a common Zulu saying is *"umuntu ngumuntu ngabuntu"* (a person is a person through other persons)

Umtata – a town in the Eastern Cape Province of South Africa

Victoria Mxenge – renowned human rights lawyer murdered in 1985

XDR-TB – the abbreviation for extremely drug resistant tuberculosis

Zonnebloem – "sunflower" in Afrikaans

ABOUT THE POET

Donna Katzin is the founding Executive Director of Shared Interest, a social investment fund that provides low-income black communities with access to capital and technical support for economic development in South and Southern Africa. Since 1994, the fund helped to move mainstream financial institutions to lend to communities of color for the first time.

She previously directed the South Africa and International Justice Programs for the Interfaith Center on Corporate Responsibility—working with institutional investors and community organizations to exert economic pressure to end apartheid, promote responsible reinvestment, and advance social criteria for domestic and international lending.

Ms. Katzin has worked as a union and community organizer and has taught at the City University of New York. She holds a master's degree in Community Organization and Planning and a doctorate in Human Services Education and Development. Her poems have appeared in journals and books, including *Crux: A Conversation in Words and Images—South Africa to South USA.*

ABOUT SHARED INTEREST

With the fall of apartheid, Shared Interest was established in 1994 as a not-for-profit vehicle to enable international investors to participate in building a more equitable South Africa—and a model to unlock commercial credit around the world for economically disenfranchised businesses and communities.

Focusing on underserved black rural and township residents, Shared Interest guarantees loans by mainstream South African financial institutions to high-impact microfinance institutions, emerging enterprises, cooperatives, and affordable housing organizations. In so doing, it moves large commercial lenders to alter their perceptions, practices, and products, and to extend credit to people and enterprises they would otherwise consider "unbankable."

In collaboration with the Swiss NGO Rafad (Recherches et Applications du Financement Alternatif au Développement), Shared Interest launched the Thembani International Guarantee Fund—today its partner in placing and monitoring guarantees and in providing technical assistance to both beneficiaries and banks.

Since inception, Shared Interest's guarantees have enabled low-income black entrepreneurs and communities to launch small and microenterprises, create and maintain jobs, and build and improve affordable homes—benefiting more than two million struggling South Africans.

ACKNOWLEDGMENTS

I am deeply indebted to a virtual community of contributors, hopeful that this book will connect at least some of them:

The dedicated directors and staff of Shared Interest and its true and tireless South African partner—the Thembani International Guarantee Fund—and to the visionary investors and supporters who have championed and sustained this work;

The South African organizations and enterprises with which we have worked—Beehive Financial Services, Development Action Group, Hands-On Fish Farming Cooperative, Bethlehem Farmers' Trust, Khula Sizwe, Kuyasa, Makhoba Trust, Norufin, Siboshwa, Small Enterprise Foundation, Tropical Mushrooms, Women's Development Bank—whose leaders', workers', and clients' voices resonate through these pages;

Archbishop Emeritus Desmond Tutu, Danny Glover, and Susan L. Taylor, who inspired and encouraged this undertaking and generously agreed to co-chair Shared Interest's Campaign for the Next Generation;

My parents, who showed me how to seek my humanity in the humanity of others, and who encouraged and made it possible for me to pursue my passions;

My godmother, Irene Eaglin, who taught me about South Africa from the time I was three and instilled a commitment to racial and economic justice and human rights;

My husband, Alan, daughter, Sari, and son, Daniel, who have helped me find my own voice and who demonstrate daily the enduring power of love;

The prophetic photographers—principally Dr. Peter Magubane, whose images for generations have shared so much of South Africa's struggle and soul;

The midwives of this manuscript—Cheryl Boyce-Taylor and Patricia Hinds—whose skilled and gentle hands have brought this book into being.

PHOTOGRAPHY CREDITS

Cover Kennet Havgaard/
Aurora Photos/
Corbis

8 Mike Hutchings/
Reuters/Corbis

16 Donna Katzin

18 Ron Haviv/VII/Corbis

20 Paul Piebinga/
Photodisc/Getty Images

22 Selwyn Tait/Sygma/
Corbis

24 Peter Magubane

26 Peter Magubane

28 Peter Magubane

30 Roger De La Harpe/
Gallo Images/Corbis

32 Bettmann/Corbis

34 Donna Katzin

36 George Steinmetz/
Corbis

39 Donna Katzin

40 Donna Katzin

42 Donna Katzin

44 Gideon Mendel/Corbis

46 Donna Katzin

48 Mariella Furrer/*The
New York Times*/Redux

50 Donna Katzin

52 Peter Johnson/Corbis

54 Donna Katzin

56 Gideon Mendel/Corbis

58 Peter Magubane

60 Donna Katzin

62 AFP/Getty Images

64 Siphiwe Sibeko/
Reuters/Corbis

66 Nic Bothma/epa/Corbis

68 Roger De La Harpe/
Gallo Images/Corbis

70 Donna Katzin

72 Donna Katzin

74 Donna Katzin

76 Donna Katzin

78 Donna Katzin

81 Donna Katzin

82 Donna Katzin

88 Shared Interest